AF431823

ERIC BLANCHARD

Fort Worth Poetry Society
Poetry Society of Texas
2022

For all those who did not heed the warning.

ACKNOWLEDGMENTS

Grateful acknowledgment is made to the journals and anthologies in which these poems, some of them in earlier versions, first appeared:

Autumn Sky Poetry: "So I Can Feel"

Burningword Literary Journal: "Inspiration" and "Morning Breath"

Common Threads (an anthology published by the Ohio Poetry Association): "Good Girls Wear Tats"

Hanging Moss Journal: "Young Rose"

Mock Turtle Zine: "All of a Sudden, but Not," "An *Ubi Sunt* for the Bees," "Beware of Poet," and "Not Quite Emo"

Oak Bend Review: "Publish Me"

Ohio Poetry Day: Best of 2012 (the contest anthology from Ohio Poetry Day): "The night could be wrong"

Poems From the Far Hills (an anthology of work by the Wright Library Poets, published by Wright Memorial Public Library, Dayton, Ohio): "Poem in My Pocket"

Poetry Quarterly: "Identity Crisis" and "Not the Dregs"

Pudding Magazine: "And God . . . ," "Frost on the Ocean," "Ode to a Sidewalk," "Old No. 2," and "This Poem Is Not" (as "This Poem")

Rust + Moth: "Wild Empathy"

Third Wednesday Magazine: "I feel naked—"

Touch: The Journal of Healing: "Needle and Spoon"

Contents

i.

Young Rose

Bud—
a firm drop of blood
on dragon bush,
blooming.

Soft complexion.
(Blush.)
Jagged edges.
Tears of dew.

Sharp fingers
caress a slender neck.
Suddenly,
a gift.

So I Can Feel

Do not give me love,
for love is hard to hold on to.
Give me a lover instead,
so I can revel in her touch
and taste her lemon skin.
Give me sweat
dripping from her curves
and the scent.
Give me the tangled limbs
and the screaming.
Give me the gentle—
the butterfly kisses
and the sighs—
so I can feel
like I have had a lover
after the spinning
and the rinsing of linen
in the morning,
when I am alone.

Wild Empathy

It must be illegal
to feed pit bulls;
they are always so skinny
and unloved,

chained in the yard.
I hear the howls.
Arrest me, if you dare.

It seems sometimes
you cannot take me anywhere.

I sob in public
at the drop of a heartbeat.

I feel the hunger
in every passing scene—
in the flash cards
and the ink blots—

and I feel the glory
after the bomb.
I have wild empathy.

I know it's just a movie,
sappy and droll,
but I cry.

An *Ubi Sunt* for the Bees

Where did all the honeybees go? The loss
of spring flowers never stung so deeply
or lingered so long. That old folksong
about young men and soldiers and flowers
          and graveyards going
          seems almost apropos.
Where did they go? To graveyards? To war?
What about weddings and rice? I will
collect birdseed, instead, for the hummingbirds
who seek flowers. I will water them with
simple syrup and iced tea (sweetened,
of course). I will attract the last
remaining bees with organic honey
generously smeared on a wooden plank.
I will cover it with glass and seal it
tightly. I will hang it on my wall,
so I can watch the bees, even after
the flowers have gone to graveyards.

Frost on the Ocean

A hundred or so paths diverged
on a great green ocean,
and looking up toward the heavens, I saw
a thousand more crisscrossing the sky.

Above those were splayed
at least a million other paths,
playful and sun bent,
lightly testing the exosphere.

As I stood, pondering whether to swim
or fly or orbit the Earth
chasing starlight,
my cortex went numb.

Frozen at the crossroad
on a brimless sea,
I did nothing. That has
certainly made a difference.

Beware of Poet

The white sign with bold lettering
has been tinged a rusty orange by weather.
It is bolted tightly to the fence.

I hung the sign to warn passers of danger.
A madman might be tossing meter and rhyme.
Beware of poet! Now you know; you've been told.

The rantings could be endless. The sputtering—
the muttering—could last deep into the night.
Don't get too close; you could catch it.

You might feel an urge to alliterate,
chase syntax, like squirrels, play whack-a-mole.
Beware of poet! Don't get too close.

You may find yourself on a road less traveled.
You might become enamored with
the way words sound . . . and then the ethos.

There is pathos unleashed in the yard,
and it could envelop your soul, if you are not
careful. You could get slobbered on for life.

Ode to a Sidewalk

Steam rises in wisps
after the afternoon sun shower.
The Ginkgo stains you
with its stench.

Dogs sniff and piss on you.
Your cracks kill mothers
by breaking backs, if
children stumble.

Colored-chalk tattoos,
hopscotch boxes.

You take us all
where we are going,
even when we wander
for hours. Well-groomed
or shaggy around the edges,
it doesn't matter.

We know that we need you,
so traffic does not tread
on our souls.

Poem in My Pocket

The poem in my pocket is a little gray mouse.
I found it early this morning, wandering
casually around the house.

It jumped into my pocket sans warning
and whispered in my ear,
Take me with you.

I did not know it was "poem-in-your-pocket"
or "take-your-mouse-to-work" day.

Of course, it may have just looked like a mouse.
It might have been a miniature
miniature Chihuahua
code-named Brutus, or Cesar Romero,
or Spot.

Out, damned spot! Out, I say!
It does not heed my Shakespearean plea—
the mousy Chihuahua stays.

I feel naked—

sitting at Starbucks alone
with my lost thoughts
down around my ankles,

and my dangling
participles, my split
infinitives, and every Oxford
comma twerking away
in my margins
to a dystopic rhythm
with a missing meter.

I've got absolutely nothing on,
nothing going on, save this
run-on composition

pretending to be
a stream of streaming consciousness,
set free from free association,

another meditation on
virtues and vices—
a series of self-righteous,
random, rambling rants,

mere diatribe and gibberish—
more drivel—than
mental gymnastics.

Good Girls Wear Tats

> *Living is easy with eyes closed,*
> *misunderstanding all you see.*
> —Lennon/McCartney

A dagger thrusts through
the heart she wears on her thigh.

The blade of her left shoulder
wears a mask shedding tears while another laughs.

Roses and fire are climbing
every curve. I try to count them all.

Sharks frenzy around her forearm.
The razor on her wrist reminds me

that danger is everywhere.
(I have counted seven, so far.)

I want to love like she does.
I want to be fearless, even after.

        I've been told
that all good girls go to heaven,
someday.

A line or two from Shakespeare
twists syntax and bears witness.

From the small of her back,
scripture swears salvation.

She's a tome that holds the answers
to everything, if only

you study her from cover to cover.
You might find some Beatles, too.

13

ii.

Not the Dregs

I scrape the bottom of the barrel,
after the top-shelf choices are gone,
to get to the sweet stuff—
          not the dregs, the molasses.

And umami—
          the oh-so savory leftovers
scavenged from midlife's
3 a.m. breakfast buffet.

Even the salty crumbs
at the bottom of the potato chip bag
set saliva aflutter,
          à la Pavlov's K9.

The good stuff separates
and falls like flakes of pure gold
in an old San Francisco saloon—
the debris, the essence.

Old No. 2

This tiny pencil has seized control.
It guides my tortured scribbling—
a primitive reminder that
even my style is old, archaic, passé.

Why this pencil? And why
not an energy-laden keyboard or keypad?
I will txt my nxt poem on twitter.
"omg! r u kidn me?"

This utensil is almost alive,
virtually buzzing with vital inspiration.
But it is merely a 3-inch stub, and
the ancient eraser is bare.

I have sharpened this pencil
at least a dozen times with my little Swiss army,
and I have begun to squeeze
rubber from its collar, like toothpaste.

As long as this gnawed-on pencil
(this forgotten bit of wood) draws breath
. . . "As long as it breathes," I whisper,
I need not fire, the wheel, sliced bread.

The night could be wrong

The dusk is telling us stories. They are
familiar in some ways, but it seems
the names have been changed to protect
the witnesses. And I thought the wind
was blowing slightly at the beginning
of the one about the boy and his dog.
The creeping darkness calls it a mutt.
I clearly remember that the dog was
an Australian Shepard, and the boy was
younger. He wasn't looking for trouble,
but the grizzly found him anyway. I
don't know where that guy came from.
That is not how I remember it. The night
could be wrong about the purple hues.
It might not even be the same story,
if the dog had not saved the boy's life.
At morning, the dog died. Still, in my
mind, I remember a happily ever after.

All of a Sudden, but Not

The flat tire was a surprise (in a way),
since I thought it was merely low. Of course,
the screw sticking out between the treads
explained it.
                    But it was the windshield
that shocked me. Not only one crack, but two
or three (actually, it's three) cracks weaving
their way from one edge to another.
"Yes, it's still safe," I told you
when I saw the worry in your eyes.
But what did I know? It was only today
that I looked closely at it from the outside.

The upper corner is smashed as if
someone took a brick to it or a baseball bat,
even the trim damaged. Then you reminded me
of the day the storm came, and stones rained down
as we passed underneath the railway tracks.
That is when it dawned on me: I should
be paying closer attention to things.

Not Quite Emo

Death wears a camo jacket
and combat boots,
not much else. Her hair
is pitch over pale
complexity—
eyes sharply lined and shining,
pout painted red.

She casts a gothic shadow, reaping
prolonged public glances
and double takes.

      When Death cuts,
it is not herself
the scythe slashes.

Death does not bleed.

Needle and Spoon

for Buster

This is how we . . .
envelop in our arms, smother
with smooches and nuzzle.

Pull loose skin from endoskeleton,
stick the steel spike in.
Stay still
while the saline bag
empties.

Watch darting eyes
succumb to numbness, until
the slow
drip
stops.

Throw a ball. He
jumps and growls. We
laugh and smile

for as long as he has energy
or until it is time to feed him.

Fickle, like an infant,
he must be coaxed with airplane noises,

plying tiny spoonful
after hopeful tiny spoonful,
until he
will no longer eat.

This is how we cope—my
addiction—since cancer has claimed
both appetite and vigor.

Conquest

I should have taken you
while I had your red dress
above your blue hair.

I should have
entered your borders and laid
claim to your defenses.

But you sighed and said
it would be like conquest,

      just before
you flew across the country

and build new bridges
and set down shoes.

I should have ransacked you,
but I did not. I should have
turned you over

and held you. Alas,
the high road holds no honor.
I showed quarter.

I let my guard down. That
is when I conceded,

      just before
you flew across the country

and unpacked baggage,
booty unclaimed.

Something Romantic

She wants something romantic,
but I am all I have.
So, we reminisce about our first kiss
that weekend in the city.

Recall holding hands
instinctively, as we amble
through the museum
like old friends.

She wants passion, so I
brush strands from her eyes
and suck sweet sweat
from her nape, nip

at her earlobes. She
musses my hair. I turn her over—
take her upstairs
for a nap.

She wants a connection. I
tell her the truth
about fear. She wants
hopes and dreams. I

share everything I know. We
agree to disagree, but we
still hold hands.
It seems we can't let go.

Morning Breath

After sleeping
for hours, I am still waiting
to exhale
          morning breath,

so I can spit
into my bathroom sink
with a healthy squeeze
          of toothpaste.

I breathe in again
          and hold it again,
like noxious-fumes avoidance
or a breakfast bong hit.

I waste scant time
gargling mouthwash
          like pickle shots,
popping placebos like Xanax,

sucking fresh air,
changing my paradigm,
changing the font
          on my nameplate,

changing my password
to something less accessible
          but honest,
changing reality itself.

I am frantic to exhale
          and spit.
Because, in the morning,
I gasp for breath.

How to write a modern poem

Write as many words as you possibly can
in one sitting or
constantly over your
entire lifetime.

Take the first line
and the last
and put them together
          carefully.

Use one or two lines
from somewhere in the middle
as the punch line.

Read it aloud
with your voice trembling.
Or shout it! Slam it
to the ground.

Turn it over and over.
Add a few more lines, and
remove a comma.
Put it all back.

Don't worry if no one gets it.
It's poetry, for Pete's sake.
Nobody has to get it.

Put it in your pocket. It's
not like you're getting paid.

iii.

And God . . .

rolling around the universe
like a pinball, bumps
off bumpers, rings
the bells, flashes
the light bulbs, spins
out of control, falls
through the hole
past flippers.

And the man
pounds his fists
and kicks at the stars
and the mystery.

The whole thing
goes tilt.

Game over.

Obligatory Insomnia Poem

I woke early this morning
to have a cup of coffee
so I could go back to bed. I am
so tired I can't sleep.

My eyes won't stay shut.
They barely blink.
My leg won't stay still. I am
tired. I can't sleep.

My mind has been running—
the hamster on a wheel
in a cage in the night. I am
so tired I can't sleep.

The coffee seems to help.
My pillow begins to comfort me.
The clock strikes six. I am
so tired.

Inspiration

A blank page is inspiration—

the silent beckoning
in a mind's ears.
          Listen.

It is just like the ocean's coy whisper
in a conch shell,
          whooshing.

A toddler scampers across it,
leaving word-like footprints.

Lacking social concerns,
he builds sandcastles

of random syllables.
Unwittingly,

the waves grow toward
tsunami,

wash away innocence,

replace it with complex
tortured syntax

and scamper away.

This Poem Is Not

This poem is not about letting go.
It is not about climbing green mountains
or diving into the blue. It is
not about you. This poem
is about kneeling down
to pet a dying dog's belly
in her waning hour. It is
about celebrating life
and drinking the wine,
about tilting at rainbows,
not only for golden windmills,
but also, for truth. This poem
is neither happy nor sad. It is
not indifferent or unchanging.
This poem is not. It is.

Publish Me

Wrap me in your critic's arms.
Edit me only slightly.

Roll me into full-color glossy.
Treat me newspaper cheap.

Spread my tender lines.
Feel my imagery.

I am an easy poem.
Publish me.

There Is No *I* in Poetry

But there is a *P*. For me,
it should almost always be
capitalized and majestic—
the reason for all things.
Wait. That might be the *o*
which comes next. Though
it is small, it is the end
of all things—the omega.
On the other hand, *e*
could stand for "everything,"
but it should probably
represent the capital-e Earth
(our entire world) or even
simply the lower-case earth—
soil to nourish life's beauty.
Then, let *t* stand for truth.
It fits it to a t—perfectly,
the likeness of a crucifix,
crossroads on life's byway.
Of course, *r* is for romance,
right? For what is Poetry
without it? Indeed, what is life
without it? And, finally,
there is *y*, because *why?* is often
an unanswered question.

Identity Crisis

I'm growing my hair long again,
because I'm a beatnik.
I'm a hippie.

I'm going to be late for work.
I have a meeting.

I'm smoking pot
and playing jazz
on my roller-disco boom box.

I am writing poetry,
instead of brushing my teeth.

I'm wearing all black.
I have a soul patch
and dark sunglasses.

My coffee is getting cold.
My dress socks don't match.

I am wearing tie-dye
and twisting daisies into dreadlocks.
I wear bell-bottom blue jeans.

I have lost my monkey suit.
I have lost my monkey.

I'm a steampunk unicorn.
I'm a hipster butterfly.

The Glove

It is springtime in Ohio—
April 1st—and, like a fool,
I battle the wind.

I battle the whipping wind
without a winter coat. It
slaps me in the face
        like a challenge,

like an assaultive glove
preceding a duel to the death—
me against the weather,

out of my element. I swear
I devoutly observed the equinox
and sacrificed
        my warm clothes

(my sweaters of wool,
my sweaters made of virgin wool)
and, still, April is cruel,

not due to blooming lilacs,
sad memories, or latent desires,
not due to the dull roots.

        But because
the welcomed spring showers
that yesterday brought flowers
today has turned to sleet.

I'm Not Picky

All I want is a grilled cheese—
nothing fancy, white bread

and Velveeta will do. And a chocolate
milk shake. Okay,

it doesn't have to be
chocolate, but

make it thick and hard to stir,
so I can let it melt a little.

Yes, smoked Gouda sounds good
on fresh sourdough or rye.

I'm not picky . . . but
sizzle up a ground-chuck patty,

medium rare and juicy.
Throw that sucker

on there, too.
You may as well include

crispy strips of bacon.
And a slice of onion. Add pickles.

Just so you know,
I put mayo on everything.

Add a basket of curly fries,
lightly salted. Also, why don't we

garnish my chocolate shake
with whipped cream?

Drizzle some chopped walnuts.
Put a cherry on top.

To A Lost Friend

I am sorry
that my joke
was offensive.

It was not
a criticism
of your love
for reading.

It was not
meant as an
overly sexual
insinuation,
          but
the ancient tome
has quite a reputation.

So, when
you sought
a recommendation
for a book
to take on
honeymoon,
I suggested
the *Kama Sutra*.

I guess
it was not
appropriate
for Facebook.

I guess
it was not
funny.